Other 'crazy' gigglebooks by Bill Stott
Cats – they drive us crazy!
Marriage – it drives us crazy!
Sex – it drives us crazy!
Rugby – it drives us crazy!

Published simultaneously in 2004 by Exley Publications Ltd in Great Britain, and Exley Publications LLC in the USA

12 11 10 9 8 7 6 5 4 3 2 1

Design by <rog@monkeyboydesign.co.uk>

ISBN 1-86187-758-7

A copy of the CIP data is available from the British Library on request.

Printed in China

Helen Exley Giftbooks, 16 Chalk Hill, Watford, Herts, WD19 4BG, UK
Helen Exley Giftbooks, 185 Main Street, Spencer MA 01562, USA
www.helenexleygiftbooks.com

A HELEN EXLEY GIGGLEBOOK

Mobiles

THEY DRIVE US CRAZY!

CARTOONS
BY BILL STOTT

PUBLIC PHONE
PUBLIC PHONE

"Ever been in one of those?"

"Oh you **must** know him – complete idiot, works in Accounts... quite often gets the same train as me. Wears a pinstripe suit and a dreadful hairpiece..."

YOU'RE BREAKING UP ..

"Look – I'm really very busy right now – text me."

101
INTERESTING
THINGS FOR
BORING PEOPLE
TO TALK ABOUT
ON THEIR
MOBILES

"I SAID, THIS IS IN CONFIDENCE. DON'T SAY A WORD TO ANYBODY!"

"Actually Darling, no, I'm not on the train anymore..."

1

2

3

4

GL R.F4 NMK POG?
NG PLFT UR FIT I 12 PQZ U

THEY'RE TALKING TEXT

"And this one's revolutionary. No useless features — can't take photos, no mindless games, and no childish ringtones. You make calls, you take calls. All it does is buzz!"

"Look at it — I hate it!
It doesn't go with my hair, my make-up,
my clothes, my handbag, or my nails..."

"They need a good clean out from time to time..."

"My phone! My phone! Is my phone hurt?"

"Yes, the cadenza's just
a tiny bit sharp..."

RINGTONE
TUNER

"You join us at a difficult time
of economies and cutbacks.
This is your mobile."

"Ha, ha, ha! Great, eh? The farting ringtone! Ha, ha, ha!"
THTHZZZPHPHT!
THTHZZZPHPHT!

BUS
STOP

"Billions of dollars spent developing videophones... for what?"

"You either need a bigger phone or your fingers sharpened..."

NO MOBILES
PASSIVE LISTENING
GETS UP YOUR NOSE
BLAH, BLAH, BLAH, BLAH, BLAH . . .

"It's a generation thing, Mom. My generation accepts all the cool things a cellphone can do. Yours doesn't."

"Oh, I can accept
things. Can it iron?"

"If the train's on time, here's when I'll be in a tunnel."

"Acme Kitchens are
in your area... and..."

CHER DOIN'?
ME TOO

CHILLIN'
COOL

"Good Lord!
So you have!"

"There've been cellphones for hundreds of years. My grandma's ringtone is by a guy called Bach and he's long dead!"

1

"So, yeah... and... yeah... it was like... so I said to him... yeah, I know... hang on a second..."

2

"Excuse me! Do you mind?
This is a private conversation!"

"Romeo, Romeo, wherefore
art thou, Romeo?
Hang on a minute..."

"Ooh, Karen! Darren talks text!"

"Well come on! We're all dying to know! Will Clive confront Dawn? Does she care? Is the promotion strings-free? Can you trust Gavin?"

"I'm bored, Ferris. Ring me up."

YOU HAVE REACHED DESERTRESCUE SERVICES. ALL OUR OPERATORS ARE BUSY.....

THE AVERAGE MOBILE SIGNAL IS GENERATED FROM A MERE 6 WATTS. I READ THAT IN A BOOK...

1

WHAT'S A BOOK?

"Great Heavens, this is going to wreck a few theories!"

"Here's the phone... and that's the operating manual!"

"The carpet's down! Great!
Have you seen my pho...?"

"My phone battery's been flat for months, but I still have loud, boring conversations on the train..."

"Ah! Beethoven's little-known harp concerto — it's mine I think."

"Sad isn't it. He leaves himself important-sounding messages in strange accents, then plays them back when he thinks everybody's listening..."

WHAT DOES YOUR PHONE MEAN TO YOU?
I CAN HANG OUT, TALKIN' TO FRIENDS.

1

WHAT DID YOU DO BEFORE YOU HAD A PHONE?
HUNG OUT, TALKIN' TO FRIENDS, ONLY CLOSER.

2

"Nope. No signal... but the games are working fine!"

HI! GREAT TO SEE YOU! IT'S BEEN AGES!

"This is the smallest cellphone ever. And that's so you don't lose it."

"Anyway, got to go... my battery's flat."

"Sorry Luv..."

"I think it's serious.
They're using a
dual charger..."

"I said, we don't
talk any more..."

"Pass the salt..."

YOU ARE CHARGED WITH STEALING MOBILE TELEPHONES HOW DO YOU PLEAD?

DIDDLE EE
DIDDLE EE
DIDDLE EE

"That's better.
You were saying?"

"Dad's making calls on his TV remote again..."
"Hello? Hello?"

"Hang on, I'm getting interference from my piercings..."

"Hi Ralph! Look, I died and went to Heaven ... haven't found a recharger yet, so give me a call soon..."

About Bill Stott

Bill Stott is a freelance cartoonist whose work never fails to pinpoint the absurd and simply daft moments in our daily lives. Originally Head of Arts faculty at a city high school, Bill launched himself as a freelance cartoonist in 1976. With sales of 2.8 million books with Helen Exley Giftbooks, Bill has an impressive portfolio of 26 published titles, including his very successful *Spread of Over 40's Jokes* and *Triumph of Over 50's Jokes*.

Bill's work appears in many publications and magazines, ranging from the *The Times Educational Supplement* to *Practical Poultry*. An acclaimed after-dinner speaker, Bill subjects his audience to a generous helping of his wit and wisdom, illustrated with cartoons drawn deftly on the spot!

What is a Helen Exley giftbook?

This little cartoon book is just one of many hilarious books available from Helen Exley Giftbooks, all of which make special gifts. We try our best to bring you the funniest jokes because we want every book we publish to be great to give, great to receive.

HELEN EXLEY GIFTBOOKS creates gifts for all special occasions – not just birthdays, anniversaries, weddings and Christmas, but for those times when you just want to say 'thanks' or 'I love you'. Why not visit our website, www. helenexleygiftbooks.com, and browse through all our present ideas?

ALSO BY BILL STOTT

Marriage – it drives us crazy!
Cats – they drive us crazy!
Rugby – it drives us crazy!
Sex – it drives us crazy!

Information on all our titles is also available from
Helen Exley Giftbooks, 16 Chalk Hill, Watford WD19 4BG, UK. Tel 01923 250505
Helen Exley Giftbooks, 185 Main Street, Spencer MA 01562, USA. Tel 877 395 3942